Ginger

A Source Book of Horses and Ponies

in the process of natural selection by imposing his own ideas and breeding selectively for a specific purpose such as racing or draught work. The simplest form of selective breeding is, of course, the natural process of the survival of the fittest: the bigger, stronger and better-equipped specimens will survive while the weaker specimens die out.

The Ice Ages accounted for the dying out of many animals, including some species of the horse; disease was also responsible; the cave man, using horse herds as a convenient source of relatively easily-obtained food, accounted for many more. No horses survived in America, and none were seen in the American continent until many thousands of years later — not, in fact, until they were taken there by the *Conquistadores* in the sixteenth century.

Of the horses that did survive, four main types eventually emerge, each being generally related to its specific environment. One of these was a pony similar to Przewalski's wild horse, averaging about 12 hands in height, and probably greyish-dun in colour with a dark eel-stripe down the centre of its back. This breed does in fact still exist in a wild state in limited numbers in the regions of Mongolia and China. The dorsal eel-stripe, as seen for instance on the native British Highland pony, is one of the very oldest markings, and for it to reappear in our present breeds with the regularity that it does, it must have a considerable degree of prepotency. Bar markings on the legs is another primeval marking still occasionally seen today — again principally on the Highland pony, one of the oldest of the British breeds. Another survivor of the Ice Ages was a heavier, more solid type averaging about 13 to 14 hands with a big heavy head, not too unlike our present Highland pony in appearance. There was also a larger, though similar type of up to 15 hands and with a big Roman nose. The last survivor was a type known as the Tarpan, about 12 hands in height and finer and lighter in build, being similar to a small Arab.

These four types spread over the land masses; the damper, colder climatic regions became hosts to the thicker, heavier, bigger types of horses, which grew thick coats, while the hot, dry, tropical parts of the world were favoured by the smaller, lighter breeds with fine coats. Thus the breeds developed into what we know as the 'cold-bloods'; the big, heavy breeds which inhabited the colder countries and the 'hot-bloods', today recognized as the Arab and also the Thoroughbred, a very recent breed. In this earlier context, 'hot-blood' refers to the Oriental horses of Turkey, Syria and Bactria as well as the Arabian.

Despite the assertions of the renowned expert, Lady Wentworth, that the Arab horse was created as a separate, undefiled race; it is obvious that the Arab, like any other breed, is as much a product of evolutionary processes, albeit a superior one, as any other living thing. Lady Wentworth claimed that the Arab was known as far back as 5000 BC and that it had its origin solely in the Arabian peninsula, but this, together with the claim that the first of the horses to be captured was owned by a great-grandson of Noah, can be largely discounted.

The Arab has been connected with the Moslem religion for many thousands of years, and Mohammed himself, realizing the importance of raising the standard of horses to make them faster and more useful when waging war against neighbouring tribes, placed obligations on his followers to improve and care for horses, promising them paradise in the next life if they bred and trained horses for the glory of God in this one. Under these conditions, 'the supreme blessing' of the Koran, the Arab horse flourished and five distinct strains, known as the Khamsa, emerged. The Kehilan was the oldest strain; the others were called Seglawi, Abeyan, Hadban and Hamdani.

Mohammed had requested that after his death his religion should be carried throughout the world, and the Arab horse was the obvious transporter of his wishes. Consequently, after his death

A Source Book of
Horses and Ponies

**Written and compiled by
Jennifer Baker**

WARD LOCK LIMITED · LONDON

Introduction

The history of the horse begins with the beginning of that of man, and all through man's development the horse has been an integral part of his progress. It has played a far greater part than any other animal in the story of civilization.

This book attempts to provide a guide to all the main breeds and types of horse and pony to be found today in different parts of the world. The general section on the development of the horse traces its history from the ancestors of sixty million years ago through to the establishment by carefully controlled breeding of today's modern breeds. The Thoroughbred is an example of a breed consciously developed by man; most breeds, however, adopted their own particular characteristics to suit their environment.

The individual entries give a very brief description of how the breed was established. The conformation of any horse is very largely what determines its successful performance, and the appearance of each breed or type is analysed as well as its particular characteristics and temperament. Obviously, however, no two horses are exactly alike, and it has therefore been necessary to generalize about the qualities of any particular breed.

I have included some of the most widespread and popular sporting activities involving the horse, as well as giving space to some of the occupations the horse has pursued, and continues to pursue, in the service of man. The accompanying illustrations enable a visual comparison between breeds to be made, and show horses performing some of the activities described in the text.

The book has been arranged alphabetically by breed, with cross-references to other entries where necessary. Instead of an alphabetical index, at the end of the book a list of entries will be found arranged under the area or country of origin of each breed. A brief survey of the Olympic Games, in which equestrian sports now play a major part, has also been included.

Evolution and Development of the Horse

The principal factor governing the evolution and distribution of the world's breeds of horses and ponies is the varying environment in which they live. The different climatic conditions, the types of soil — and therefore the foliage and herbage growing there — the water supply and the accessibility or otherwise of available food all help to determine the size, hardiness, speed and inherent characteristics of the horse.

Approximately sixty million years ago, Eohippus, the little 'dawn horse' which is acknowledged as being the direct ancestor of our present-day horse, wandered freely throughout Europe, Asia and the Americas; the level of the sea was considerably lower then than now and the main land masses were all connected. Eohippus was about the size of a fox, with four toes on each forefoot and three toes on each hind. He was small because food was scarce and consisted mainly of stunted shrubs; and with the generally swamp-like conditions underfoot he was better served by pads,

similar to a dog's foot, which could spread, than he would have been by hooves, which would sink in the marshy ground.

Mesohippus and Miohippus are the next in succession. They both had only three toes in front and three behind, and had by now grown to about the size of a sheep. The land was beginning to dry up and grass started to make an appearance on the patches of open ground; the 'horse' was developing stronger teeth in order to cope with this new form of herbage.

About ten million years ago Pliohippus and later Hipparion made their appearance. They were larger, about the size of a donkey, and only the middle one of their three toes remained in contact with the ground. Fossils of Hipparion have been found throughout Africa as well as in Europe and Asia, and it must be assumed, therefore, that the species extended over these areas.

The remaining significant factor affecting the evolution of the horse is the interference of man in AD 632 the Arab spread throughout the desert and North Africa into Europe, and has ever since had the greatest influence on all European breeds.

With the spread of the Arab through Africa, Europe and Asia will be seen the emergence of the third type of horse which we know, the 'warm-blood', the result of the crossing, by the influence of man or the inclination of nature, of the hot-blooded Oriental with the heavier cold-blood type of horse.

With the invasion of the Moors into Spain — an invasion that reached well into Europe and was only halted by their decisive defeat at Poitiers in 732 by the armoured horsemen of Charles Martel — came the foundation of the Andalusian horse. Many of the Barb horses, the mounts of the Moors, were left behind after these invasions, and over the centuries they crossed with the local equine inhabitants. The resultant Spanish Andalusians were to have a considerable influence in Europe.

Meanwhile, the Battle of Hastings in 1066 launched, as far as horses are concerned, the start of the Middle Ages. Contrary to popular opinion, horses were at this time probably no more than about 15 hands in height. Knights were protected by light chain mail, giving a total weight of rider and saddle of perhaps sixteen stone. In the First World War, the British cavalry horse was expected to carry between seventeen and eighteen stone. It was not until the end of the Middle Ages, with the development of the plate-armour, that the heavy carthorse type, the Great Horse, emerged. In fact, Richard Coeur de Lion on the Third Crusade rode Oriental Turkoman horses.

During the time of the Crusades, at the beginning of the thirteenth century, battles and tournaments were introduced to provide knights with the excitement of war without the discomforts attached to it. This was the beginning of the age of chivalry, which was to continue until the end of the century. As more effective weapons, in the form of the longbow, appeared on the scene, protective covering in the form of plate-armour began to be worn, first by the knights themselves, and later to protect the horses too. One effect of this was that, in order to carry approximately thirty stone of armour, saddle and knight, much bigger, weight-carrying horses had to be bred and so the Great Horse developed. Eventually infantry took over the role of the war horse, but the tournament continued to flourish as a spectator sport. The heavily armoured knights no longer used the tournaments as practice for war, and the idea of chivalry waned accordingly. Musical rides, parades, displays of horsemanship and tilting the quintain for which active, lighter horses were of far more use, became the fashionable pastimes.

It was at this stage that the Andalusian came into his own. His eye-catching action, elevated trot, elegant walk and proud bearing made him the mount of kings and princes, the élite of the horse world, for centuries. Most of the royal court studs

of Europe based their breeding on the Andalusian because of his supreme elegance, tremendous agility and overall impression of spirited animation combined with his quality good looks and docile temperament. He was the ideal manège horse, which was the only form of riding practised in Europe during the Renaissance period, the formative period of classical equitation. The Andalusian was, in fact, the founder of the present Lippizaner breed; the Archduke Charles II of Styria imported Spanish horses in 1580 and started the stud at Lippica. The early Lippizaners were often spotted, as were the early Andalusians, but in time this colouring, along with chestnuts, bays, browns and so on, was bred out by selective breeding until only the grey Lippizaners that we see today remained.

The seventeenth-century Duke of Newcastle prized the Andalusian for its natural talent and ability in *haute école*, and the baroque hall built in the garden of the palace of the Habsburgs, although supplied with Lippizaners and situated in Vienna, takes its title, the Spanish Riding School of Vienna, from the Spanish or Andalusian horses which were first used there for high-school riding. The Arab influence makes its presence felt in the Lippizaner through the Seglawi strain of Arab which founded one of the five strains of Lippizaner, the Siglavy; the other strains being Pluto, which is believed to be based on the Danish Frederickborg breed, Maestoso and Favory, based on the Kladruby breed, which in turn had Spanish blood, and Conversano and Neapolitano, imported from Italy but also based on Spanish blood. In Britain Andalusian blood was undoubtedly infused into the Connemara and Welsh breeds as well as the Cleveland Bay and the spotted horses.

Following the influence of Oriental blood in Europe, the greatest landmark in the history of horse-breeding must be the development of the Thoroughbred. The Thoroughbred is almost definitely descended from Arab sires, but there must be some doubt as to just how far the Arab is responsible for the Thoroughbred breed. It seems unlikely that the Thoroughbred was developed entirely from pure Arab on both sides, as if this was the case the Arab would surely throw replicas of himself, instead of the rather bigger, faster horse that we know as the Thoroughbred. Running horses, for instance, which were probably of Spanish origin, were imported into England in the twelfth century and Richard II had two horses which he raced in 1377 which were both almost certainly of the running-horse type.

It seems more likely, therefore, that Arab sires were put to these running-horse mares. The first matches, or races, between individual owners were run over several miles and in several heats. Organized racing in fact started at Newmarket Heath. In 1711, Queen Anne, a great sporting enthusiast, opened Ascot Park to racegoers and racing was regularly featured there. Hunting, too, was very popular all over Europe, especially in England and France, the wolf, wild boar and red and fallow deer being the subject of the chase. Again, running horses were almost definitely used to mount the followers of the chase.

The imported Arab founders of the Thoroughbred were the Byerley Turk, a direct ancestor of the Tetrarch and Herod lines; the Darley Arabian, founder of the Eclipse, St Simon and Flying Childers strains; and the Godolphin Arabian whose descendants were Matchem and Man O'War.

The Byerley Turk was foaled in 1680 and was brought back to England from Hungary in 1684. He had been acquired by Colonel Byerley, who was fighting the Turks there. He was later used as Colonel Byerley's charger at the Battle of the Boyne. The Darley Arabian, originally named Manak, was one of the Muniqi strain of Arabs. He was foaled in 1700 and brought back by Thomas Darley in 1705. The Godolphin Arabian did not arrive in England until 1730; originally named El Sham, he had been given to Louis XV of France by the Sultan of Morocco together with seven other horses. The Arab was not suitable for *haute école* riding and he was sold, eventually finding himself pulling a greengrocer's cart in Paris. He was bought by Edward Coke, who brought him back to England and subsequently gave him to his friend Lord Godolphin to use as a 'teaser' on his Derbyshire stud. A chance mating proved El Sham's worth when two colt foals by him, Lath and Cade, over a period of five years beat all comers at the Newmarket races.

It was not until 1793, with the founding of the General Stud Book, that the Thoroughbred became an established breed. Today, however, the Thoroughbred is taking over from the Arab in the upgrading of the European warm-bloods, although there are some instances, particularly with some of our native breeds, where Arab blood is more suitable for upgrading than Thoroughbred.

The first horses to land in America after their

disappearance from that continent during the Ice Ages, were eleven stallions and five mares probably of Andalusian or Arab blood. They were brought ashore on the coast of Mexico in 1509 by Hernan Cortez who used them as cavalry horses. From this beginning they spread over the American continent. The origin of the Mustangs of North America can be attributed to an adventurer by the name of Hernando de Soto. Thirty years after Cortez' conquest, de Soto set off from Florida in search of gold, taking two hundred horses with him. By the time his expedition reached the Mississippi there were only forty surviving horses, and as these were in very poor condition it was decided to kill them off for meat. Five of the horses, however, managed to escape and these are supposed to be the founders of the herds of Mustangs which roamed the Western prairies.

In 1680 during the Spanish massacre in New Mexico by the Apache Indians from the west and south, many horses were killed and the rest captured by the Apaches, who soon became skilful horsemen. Horses soon spread north across the plains through Utes, Pawnees and Comanches to the Canadian border. In due course, the looted Spanish horses crossed with the Mustangs of the prairies and a new type of pony emerged, the cayuse, about 13 hands in height, intelligent, remarkably tough and notoriously hard and sound — a direct link with its Arabian ancestors. The Indians used these ponies as mounts for their hunting escapades and when waging war on neighbouring tribes.

The only tribes who bred horses selectively were the Nez Percé Indians, who lived in the region of the Palouse river and developed the Appaloosa, principally from the Spanish horses. The Nez Percé were finally wiped out by the United States cavalry in 1877 after a series of battles, but their horses have remained popular to this day.

When the French, English and Dutch immigrants settled in Canada and Virginia, they brought with them the horses they had used at home to work their farms and to ride, and more new breeds developed. The Narragansett Pacer was perhaps one of the most popular types to emerge, as he was remarkably fast and comfortable for covering long distances, but he became extinct by the eighteenth century, having become so popular that demand had far exceeded supply.

The Quarter Horse of America got its name from the quarter-mile races that were held along the one straight stretch of roadway through the middle of towns. The breed probably descended from a combination of the Spanish horses and a Thoroughbred stallion, Janus, who was imported in 1752; the horses were constantly being up-graded by using Thoroughbred stock to improve the quality of the breed.

In 1795 Justin Morgan, a native of Vermont, was given a bay Thoroughbred two-year-old colt in payment of a debt. He named the colt Figure, used him as a general all-round horse on the farm and for riding, and won a few races with him. A small horse, only about 14 hands, he was believed to be by the stallion True Briton, and was possessed of extraordinary strength and toughness, as well as speed and endurance. He had the Arabian head, high head and tail carriage and was an exceptionally willing all-rounder.

By selective breeding from the Morgan horse, as Figure later became known, and from Quarter Horses, a three-gaited horse, the Tennessee Walking Horse, emerged. The three gaits are an ordinary walk, an easy canter and a high-stepping running-walk which covers the maximum ground with the minimum of effort. Similar to the Tennessee Walking Horse but with an ordinary trot in place of the running-walk are the American Saddlebred and Standardbred horses, both of Thoroughbred ancestry, the latter being a fine trotter.

In a very short space of time America has developed an extraordinary number of horses, based originally on the imported Spanish stock, and with later importations of Arab and Thoroughbred blood, all of which have evolved and developed their own particular characteristics to cope with their environment and the uses to which mankind has put them.

All over the world, horses and ponies are increasingly being used for leisure and sporting activities, a balancing factor in a situation where their value as working animals has diminished with the advent of mechanization. Since the Second World War, in particular, there has been a really remarkable upsurge of interest in all aspects of horses and horsemanship which shows every sign of continuing to grow.

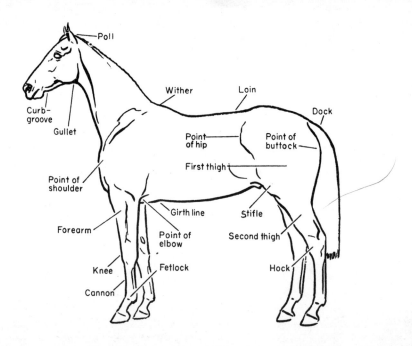

Poll

Wither

Loin

Dock

Curb-groove

Gullet

Point of hip

Point of buttock

First thigh

Point of shoulder

Girth line

Stifle

Forearm

Point of elbow

Second thigh

Knee

Fetlock

Hock

Cannon

The most important things to think about before buying a horse or pony are what you are going to ask the horse to do and what facilities you have for keeping it. There is no point in buying an expensive Thoroughbred if you have only an orchard in which to keep it and intend just to hack quietly round the lanes where you live. If, however, you want a horse that will perform creditably out hunting or at gymkhanas or an animal which you can take into the show ring, you will need to be prepared to spend more money on it when you buy it and expect a greater output in both money and effort in taking care of it.

The golden rule, where buying a horse is concerned, is never, under any circumstances, to buy an animal that is unsound, no matter how endearing it may be in other respects. It will probably be cheap to buy but it will prove exceedingly expensive in veterinary bills, and a horse you cannot ride still has to be fed and looked after.

When you are thinking of buying a particular horse, it is always wise to ask a vet to inspect it. Nowadays, vets no longer issue a general certificate of soundness: they have had to become more cautious and instead they state that on the day on which the inspection took place, from the examination that was undertaken at that time, the horse appeared to be sound and in good health. This qualification protects the vet from possible recriminations in the future. Nevertheless, an inspection by a good vet will be carried out with great thoroughness and care and it should be regarded as an essential part of buying any horse.

The conformation of a horse is a vital clue to its likely performance. Some horses are, of course, 'better' — in that their performance and potential are greater — than others, but good conformation is likely to indicate a horse that is able to perform well, and only very rarely do horses with bad conformation do well in any branch of equitation.

What is good conformation? It is not easy to define this. One of the best ways to acquire an 'eye' for a horse is to study horses in the show ring and to decide why those who win do so. This takes a considerable amount of time; it is possible, however, to fix in one's mind quite quickly a general picture of what a horse should and should not look like. Proportion is one essential ingredient of good conformation. If the head looks unduly large or the limbs unusually long, the chances are that they are out of proportion with the rest of the horse. Let us look at the individual points of the horse in slightly more detail.

The horse's head will tell you a good deal about the whole animal. The eye should be kind, and show intelligence and alertness. Small eyes, or those showing a lot of white, should be regarded with some suspicion, though they do not *always* indicate a mean or nervy type. A delicate, attractive head will indicate some quality blood in the horse, whereas heavy, coarse heads belong to more 'common' breeding. The ears, like the eyes, are an indication of temperament — rather like the mouth in humans. Are the ears pricked, responsive and mobile? If so, there is a good chance that the horse will be generally responsive, interested in what is going on and prepared to co-operate. Perhaps the most important thing about the head is that it should be set on to the neck properly and be proportionate to the size and shape of the neck and body of the horse.

The age of horses is discovered by inspecting their teeth. This is easy to do once the knowledge has been acquired, but it does take an expert to 'read' the right information.

The neck should be strong, but not too short, thick and 'cresty', for necks of this kind are often stiff. On the other hand, a long, thin neck is a weak neck, and a horse will find it difficult to carry its head in the correct position. The angle at which the neck joins the horse's body is also important, for it affects the distribution of the horse's weight. Ideally, there should be no interruption where neck and shoulder join.

The formation of the horse's withers is a vital point. Unless the wither is well formed, the shoulder is unlikely to be of the correct shape for free movement of the front limbs. The shoulder should be long, sloping, well laid back. Straight shoulders — which are generally to be found in conjunction with low, flat withers — generally indicate a short stride, which increases the strain on the forelegs and is much less comfortable for riding.

Both forelegs and hind legs in the horse should be 'clean'. The forelegs should be long in the forearm, short in the cannon, with the elbow free rather than tied in. Horses that are back at the knee or over at the knee are to be avoided as this almost always results in strains caused by weakness. Ligaments and tendons should be firm and hard, with no puffiness. The measurement of bone, taken just below the knee, is important,

though it should be remembered that an Arab horse, for example, has a greater density of bone than some other breeds and therefore the actual measurement need not be so great. Fetlocks should be flat, neither round nor fleshy. The pastern should be neither too long nor too short and upright. Both faults add to strain.

A horse is only as good as its feet, and the greatest attention should be paid to an inspection of the feet of any horse one is considering buying. The fore and hind feet should be comparable in size and shape; the wall should be strong and without any signs of cracking; heels should be deep and open; the frog healthy, large and well formed. Feet that turn out or in will affect the horse's action.

The horse's lungs need room for expansion, and the shape of the chest is therefore important. It should be wide, as a narrow chest prevents this expansion and also means that the forelegs 'come out of one hole' and are inhibited in their action;

but not too wide, for this is usually combined with heavy shoulders and chest which prevent speed. To correspond with a well-formed chest, the girth should be deep, and the ribs well sprung. The horse's back should carry a saddle well. It must not be too long, for this indicates weakness, and any abnormalities, such as a hollow back or roach back, should be avoided. Excessively short backs will show strength, but they do not make for a comfortable ride.

It is the rear parts of the horse that provide the propulsion for forward movement, and they should therefore give an appearance of power. A horse that dwindles away and looks mean will lack power so the quarters, loins and hind legs should be well developed, rounded and muscular. The hocks, like the knees, should be set low, and should ideally be in a vertical line with the point of the quarters. They should be set straight rather than turning either out or in.

Overall, then, you should look for proportion and symmetry in a horse. No horse is perfectly made, but as a general rule one that is well put together will perform better than one that is not.

When you are inspecting a horse, you should not only study its conformation but look at it in action. Have it run up in hand, both towards you and away from you, and watch its action carefully. Have it ridden by its owner, but also ride it yourself, as a horse may perform very differently for a rider it knows well and who can get the best out of it.

One does not enter into a partnership of any kind with a fellow human being whom one does not like. The same should be true of a horse you are thinking of buying. Perhaps the most important of all the questions to be considered is whether you like the horse. If so, and if it fulfils the other requirements, then you are probably right to buy it. If, however, you yourself do not like it, then however suitable it may be in other respects the chances are it will not suit you. And that, after all, is what is most important.

The Akhal-Teke is a breed of great antiquity believed to have been bred around 500 BC in Turkmenistan, where the best ones are still bred. In the Middle Ages they were imported to Russia and bred in great numbers; they are now bred in collective farms in North Caucasia. The average height is about 15.2 hands, and the breed is bay, chestnut, black and grey in colour. Typically, the head is long and thin, as is the neck. The mane and tail hair is silky. The horses are somewhat light of bone and are very narrow. They are exceptionally hardy and can endure great extremes of heat and cold. They are used extensively for jumping, racing, dressage and long-distance riding.

The Alter-Real is a native of Portugal and is descended from the Spanish Andalusian. The Alter do Chao Stud Farm was founded in 1748 and for many years the breed was kept pure. However, with the introduction of French mares, the breed tended to decline in quality and it was decided to use Arabian stallions for upgrading. The Alter-Real is usually bay or dark brown in colour, though greys are occasionally seen too, and has a broad head and large eye. He has a short neck, is close-coupled with fine bone and is both willing and obedient. Standing at 15 to 15.2 hands, he is very supple, and his extravagant action makes him ideal for *haute école*.

American Saddlebred

Originally known as the Kentucky Saddle Horse, this horse was developed from the Thoroughbred crossed at different times with Morgans and with the now extinct Narragansett Pacer. Its original purpose was to carry the planters round their plantations, and for this purpose it was necessary to have a horse who was able to work all day at a comfortable pace without tiring. It has five gaits: walk, trot, canter, slow gait — a four-beat slow prancing pace — and the rack — a much faster version of the slow gait — at which the horse can cover a mile in just over two minutes. Usually about 16 hands, Saddlebreds can be bay, black, brown, chestnut or grey; they have great 'presence', showy action and a high tail carriage, usually artificially induced.

The Andalusian originated in the Jerez de la Frontera district of Spain. It is descended from Oriental horses brought over with the Moorish invaders and later crossed with the existing Spanish ponies. The Carthusian monks bred the Andalusian at their monasteries in Jerez, Seville and Cazallo and refused to use infusions of Neapolitan blood, preferring to keep the breed pure. They were the favourite mount of the élite of the horse world from as far back as the fourteenth century. They are still bred in the Jerez region of south-west Spain, principally at the Terry Stud. Averaging 15.2 to 16 hands, they are usually grey, black, bay or brown in colour with a straight profile, thick neck, sloping shoulder and strong legs and with elegant action and proud bearing.

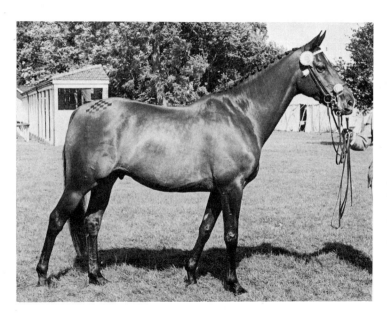

The Anglo-Arab is a cross between a Thoroughbred and an Arabian, and should combine the best qualities of both without displaying the characteristics of one breed to the exclusion of the other. With the intelligence and soundness of the Arab and the size, scope and speed of the Thoroughbred the Anglo-Arab is ideal for most activities, and has proved his value as a dressage horse, eventer and hunter as well as a good, useful all-round riding horse.

See also: French Anglo-Arab.

Although chiefly found in the western areas of the United States, Appaloosas are becoming increasingly popular throughout the country. They are descended from Spanish stock and were subsequently captured and trained by the Nez Percé Indians in the region of the Palouse river. They can be any size but are usually about 15.2 hands. Six coat-colour combinations are recognized by the Appaloosa Horse Club. Roans are the most common colouring found, usually with dark spots on a white rump, but it is quite possible to have white quarters without the spots, spots over the whole body or white spots on a dark background. Other Appaloosa characteristics are white sclera surrounding the eyes, a mottled skin, parti-coloured hooves, frequently in vertical stripes, and a rat tail.

Arabs are now bred extensively in Britain, and Arab blood has influenced the majority of our breeds at some stage. Very strong, hardy and outstandingly sound, the Arab is perhaps the most beautiful breed, with its short head, dished face, 'pint-pot' muzzle and small ears. The tail should be set high, the cannon bones short and the bone hard and dense. Tough and capable of carrying weights out of all proportion to its size, the Arab is acknowledged to be the most intelligent of all breeds. The Arabian is essentially a small breed and attempts to increase the size often result in loss of type. The Arabian makes a very comfortable riding horse, being light in front and having a natural balance. He can cover long distances at a relatively fast speed carrying a lot of weight, can jump and produce a perfectly adequate dressage test, though his particular *metier* is probably the long-distance ride. In fact, the Arab is an ideal all-round riding horse.

See also: Desert Arab, French Arab, Polish Arab, Shagya Arab.

The Ardennes is a native of Belgium and is found principally in Liège and Luxembourg. It is the older of the two breeds of draught horse in Belgium, the other being the Belgian Heavy Draught which has had some influence on the Ardennes. A solid, stocky horse, he stands 15 to 15.3 hands and is usually chestnut, roan bay or sorrel in colour. He is noted for his calm and willing nature and is especially suited to work the hilly districts of Belgium. A closely related strain of the Ardennes is also bred in Sweden.

Australian Thoroughbred

There were no horses at all in Australia when it was discovered in the sixteenth century and it was not until the eighteenth century that Europeans imported them first from South Africa and South America and later from Europe. The English Thoroughbred was imported some time later and soon became popular for racing; well over a thousand Thoroughbreds a year are now bred for this purpose.

See also: French Thoroughbred, Thoroughbred.

Bashkir

This heavy breed of Russian horse takes its name from the area where it was first bred: it is local to Bashkiria in the southern foothills of the Ural mountains. Special breeding centres were first set up in 1845 to extend the breed. It is unusual in that the mares are still bred largely for their milk, which is used in the manufacture of the drink *kumiss*. The stallions and geldings are used both for riding and driving and draught work. The Bashkir is famed for its powers of endurance: a troika of Bashkirs is said to travel up to seventy-five miles in a day over the snow.

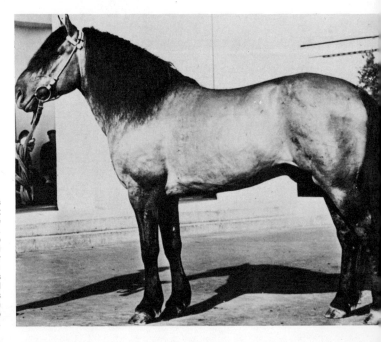

Breton

Originally bred in the Black Mountains area of the Breton peninsula in France, the Breton is a short, compact, stuffy little horse of about 15.2 hands. He has a thick neck, short legs with very little feather and is very strong and hardy with good action. The most noted colour is chestnut roan, but chestnut, bay and occasionally black are also seen. Their principal use today is as an agricultural work horse, though at one time they were used by the horse artillery.

Wild horses, otherwise known as Brumbies, roam in their hundreds the upland slopes of the Snowy River, New South Wales, as well as other regions of Australia. When caught, some of these Brumbies prove very useful and for many years they were shipped overseas as cavalry remounts. They do in the main, however, tend to be rather wild and difficult to school, and today many of them are being destroyed to save valuable grazing for cattle. They are scrub horses, descended from the domestic horse, but they have gone wild and can now be any colour and height.

Budjonny

A very recent breed, the Budjonny was bred originally for use as a cavalry horse at the cavalry army stud in the Rostov area of the USSR. He is the result of selective crossings between the best of the Don mares and Thoroughbred stallions. Standing at an average 16 hands, they are nearly always bay or chestnut in colour, are well built and have good jumping ability, combined with a placid temperament. They are now used principally for racing and endurance riding.

Bred in the poor swamplands of the Rhône delta, the pony population of the Camargue numbers about 4,000. It is a tough, hardy, weight-carrying little horse of about 14 hands whose origins are a little obscure. Some maintain that it is an indigenous breed while others attribute its origin to Asian horses. It is in fact probably one of the oldest French breeds. Always grey in colour, the Camargue has a large head and a rather short neck joining a straightish shoulder. He should be short and strong in the loins, have a lot of bone, large feet and a thick mane and tail. He is extremely strong and sure-footed, and makes a useful trekking pony.

Caspian

Rediscovered in 1965 roaming wild on the shores of the Caspian Sea in northern Iran, the Caspian pony stands between 10 and 12 hands and has the appearance of a small horse. It has a remarkable jumping ability and is very suitable for carrying a small child over rough country. They are usually bay or brown in colour, with no white markings.

The best cavalrymen of ancient times were the Scythians. They used the horse as a means of a quick getaway after having delivered their missiles, rather than for direct combat. The invention of saddle and stirrup provided the first means of direct conflict, followed by knights in plate armour and the Great Horse. Then lighter, overbent horses were taught the 'airs above the ground' which were supposed to be useful in close combat.

Cromwell realized the necessity of strict training and discipline, but Prince Rupert did not, and the cavalry galloped flat out at anything and everything 'as if the art of war were precisely the same as fox-hunting'. The Charge of the Light Brigade at Balaclava led by Lord Cardigan was a tragic farce: the enemy was never contacted but almost half the horses in the charge were killed. The standard of horsemanship throughout the Crimea was appalling and, according to Captain Mercer, 'the British Dragoon looked upon the animal as a source of perpetual drudgery to himself'. By the American Civil War, it was realized that the rifle fired at a distance was a more effective weapon than a sword or lance at close quarters; horses in the 1914–18 war became the means of transport and the officer's first consideration, not the last.

Circus Horses (1)

Circus horses can be divided into three types — 'high-school' horses, Rosinbacks and Liberty horses — depending on the displays performed. High-school horses should be quality animals with good action and plenty of bone and must have an equable temperament. They normally take between one and two years to train before being ridden in public. The Rosinback is the horse used for bareback circus riding and he gets his name from the fact that resin is rubbed into his quarters and back to prevent the performers slipping when they jump on to his back. He must be very placid and not be upset by the performers leaping all over him, vaulting on and off or hanging on to his tail. His back must be wide and level and his paces, particularly the canter, smooth and level and close to the ground. The Liberty horse is usually Arab or Anglo-Arab; for circus work the members of a team must all match in colour and size as a dozen or so are used in the ring at one time. Stallions and geldings are used in preference to mares as they have a more showy action. The normal training time is about a year; it probably takes as long to train one or two replacements in a team as it does a whole new team.

Rosinbacks must be very placid and have a smooth steady stride which is unlikely to be upset by any movements on the part of the performers. Unlike the Liberty horses, they do not need to match in colour but for displays such as this it is necessary to have them all more or less the same size. Rosinbacks are the most difficult circus horses to find as there are so many requirements to fulfil.

The Cleveland Bay is bred in north-east Yorkshire and is descended from an old breed of packhorse known as the Chapman horse. Two distinct types of Cleveland evolved from the Chapman horse. One was the result of Thoroughbred crossings and became known as the Yorkshire Coach Horse; it was much in demand in Victorian times for agricultural work. The other, bred from within the breed by selective crossings, resulted in the breed we now know as the Cleveland Bay. A big, powerful horse standing 16 to 16.2 hands, he is always bay in colour with no white markings. He should have an abundance of hard, flat bone and a good sloping shoulder.

The Cleveland Bay is a useful carriage horse as well as making a very efficient heavyweight hunter with natural jumping ability. When crossed with Thoroughbred blood a faster and lighter type of horse is produced, up to most competitive activities. They frequently make ideal eventers and show-jumpers.

Originally bred in Flanders in Belgium, some stallions were imported during the eighteenth and nineteenth centuries to improve the native breed in Clydesdale, Scotland, which is now known as Lanarkshire. Alone among British heavy horses, the Clydesdale is the possessor of plenty of power and strength without being coarse and heavy. He should have a flat face, not dished, joining a long neck and well laid back shoulder. The back should be short, the quarters long, and straight action with a long, free stride is a must. There should be an abundance of silky feather, and the feet should be hard and open. The height ranges from 16.2 to 17.2 hands; permissible colours are dark brown and black; white markings on the face and legs are encouraged.

The cob is a type of sturdy, 'stuffy' short-legged little horse, and is not a breed. He is immensely strong, and can carry the heaviest weight for a day's hunting and still be there at the end, though he is not suitable for fast grassland hunting countries. His placid temperament makes him ideal for the elderly or nervous rider. He has a short back, short legs with a lot of bone, large, well-rounded quarters, a deep body, good riding shoulder set on to a neck with a good length of rein and a large well-proportioned head with wide-set eyes. He can be any colour and there is no height limit, though the usual size is around 15 hands.

Connemara

The Connemara can claim to be Ireland's only native pony, which for a country considered to be one of the best horse-producing countries in the world is rather surprising. A sturdy, useful, general-purpose pony of between 13 and 14.2 hands, he makes a good riding pony, especially when crossed with Arab or Thoroughbred blood. These crosses have, indeed, produced such famous names as Little Model, Korbous and Dundrum. Connemaras can be grey, dun, bay, black or brown, and they are noted particularly for their tractable nature, agility and jumping ability. They are tough, sure-footed and deep through the girth, with sloping shoulders and free action.

The horses ridden for cutting out calves are usually of Quarter Horse breeding. Displays of roping calves, like this one at the Calgary Stampede, are given by the cowboys at rodeos held throughout America and Canada.

Dales

Similar to the Fell, the Dales pony is bred on the eastern side of the Pennines in County Durham, Northumberland and Yorkshire, and the two may have a common ancestry. Good in harness, the Dale is exceptionally strong and is capable of carrying or pulling great weights although his tendency to a straight shoulder makes him more suitable for driving than riding. Inherently sound, sure-footed and active, the Dales is a great trotter and is suitable for any kind of farm work. Slightly larger than the Fell, these ponies should not exceed 14.1 hands and may be black or dark brown, with an abundance of mane, tail and feather.

Dartmoor

The Dartmoor pony, found in Devonshire, is one of the oldest British breeds. A number of herds still run wild on windswept Dartmoor. Bays, blacks and browns with only a small amount of white markings are the acceptable colours for this tough little breed and the height limit is 12.2 hands. The principal characteristics of the Dartmoor are his fine, pretty head, small prick ears and good front and shoulder, combined with his intelligence and sure-footedness. An ideal child's pony with an equitable temperament, he is small and narrow enough for a young child but sufficiently versatile for an older one. Successfully crossed with a small Thoroughbred, this already good-looking pony then often makes a first-class show pony; it has contributed greatly to the production of quality children's ponies.

It is impossible to say when horses were first introduced to the Arabian desert, but the Bedouin undoubtedly saw the Arab as being a useful addition to the camel. With the lack of grazing and scarcity of water supply, both Bedouin and Arab had to be continually on the move, and in order to keep up with the camel the Arabs quickly developed their long stride. One strain of Arab bred by the Bedouin, the Muniqi, excelled as a racehorse. It resulted from crossing the Arab with the bigger Turkoman horse of Iraq. The Darley Arabian (*see* Thoroughbred) was one of these progeny. Desert Arabs rarely reach more than 15 hands, but they are always known as horses, not ponies.

See also: Arab, French Arab, Polish Arab, Shagya Arab.

The Don is the horse of the Russian steppe and was ridden by the Cossacks as far back as the eighteenth century. Originally similar to the Mongolian pony, the Don was crossed with Persian and Karabakh breeds and later with Thoroughbreds, but more recently no outside blood has been introduced. They are exceptionally hardy and live out on the steppes all year round with no supplementary food. Always chestnut in colour with a darker mane and tail, they are about 15.2 to 16 hands in height and are very useful all-round horses, being as good under saddle as in harness. They are also raced with considerable success.

The present-day domestic donkey is descended from the wild ass of Africa. It used to abound in the Sudan and in Somaliland and was much bigger than the donkey we know today. The wild asses of Asia, another strain, are dun-coloured instead of the familiar grey and the ears are smaller; it is unlikely that they had any influence on the domestic donkey. Today's donkey stands at between 10 and 11 hands, and can be grey, brown, chocolate, skewbald or a pale chestnut known as 'pink'. All have the distinctive cross-marking down the back and across the wither down to the shoulder. The coat is thick; the head large with a slight dish; there should not be any tendency to cow hocks. The donkey is self-willed but very friendly, and can be ideal as a small child's first mount or to put between shafts.

Dressage is defined as 'the systematic training of a horse for a particular purpose'. It is the stage between the breaking of a horse to saddle and the execution of the final purpose to which the horse is to be put – in other words, simply training or schooling as a means to achieve a better horse at the end. Pure dressage, however, is an end in itself and is this schooling process carried to a far more advanced stage. Domini Lawrence and San Fernando, members of the British Olympic dressage team, are here executing a very good relaxed *piaffe*. The *piaffe* is a slow, lofty, cadenced trot similar to the *passage*, but it is performed without gaining any ground. It is an extremely collected pace and is featured only in the advanced dressage tests.

Driving

Even when the only means of transport was to ride or to drive a horse, driving was a popular sport. In many countries, horse shows now hold special classes for driving enthusiasts, and cross-country drives and marathons also take place. Some breeds have been specially developed for harness work – Cleveland Bays, Friesians and Haflingers, for example. Horses can be driven in various combinations to many different vehicles, from the one-pony dog cart to a coach pulled by a team of up to twelve horses.

Exmoor

Bred in the south-western tip of Britain, in Devon and Somerset, the Exmoor has had to survive on some of the wildest and roughest moorland, and is in consequence one of the hardiest of the native breeds. There are two distinct types of Exmoor, the Acland or Anchor type, which is slightly smaller and is usually a reddish-brown colour, and the Withypool which is usually darker, larger and with a straighter profile. The height limit is 12.3 hands, and only bays, browns and a yellowish-brown dun are acceptable colours. No white markings are allowed, and the distinctive mealy muzzle and mealy colouring round the eyes must always be in evidence. The Exmoor's other principal characteristics are his close, springy coat which is virtually waterproof, and his 'toad' eye, which with surrounding hair of the right colour appears prominent. A short thick head set on to a neck with a good length of rein, well laid back shoulders, tail neatly set in, neat hard feet and free straight action, combined with strength and pony character, make the Exmoor a good all-round pony for every occasion.

Eventing

Eventing has only fairly recently become an established sport in Britain, but its rise in popularity has been rapid, and over fifty one-day events are now organized annually. An event consists of three phases: dressage, show-jumping and cross-country, which consists of perhaps three to four miles ridden across country over some twenty to twenty-five obstacles. In addition, of course, there are two three-day events. Badminton is held in April on the Duke of Beaufort's land in Gloucestershire, and the Burghley event takes place in September at the home of the Marquis of Exeter at Stamford. In addition to the other phases the three-day event even has a steeplechase course of approximately two miles with about twelve fences, and six to twelve miles of roads and tracks to complete at a steady pace. There are also rather more cross-country obstacles spread over a greater distance of up to five miles. The whole section is known as the speed and endurance phase. In a one-day event the show-jumping is held before the cross-country, whereas in a three-day event it comes at the end. An eventer is of no special breeding, but it usually has a high percentage of Thoroughbred blood to give the required speed and stamina.

The Falabella takes its name from the South American ranching family who first became interested in breeding these diminutive ponies some fifty years ago. There is still some controversy about how the breed was established, but it is known to descend from a small Thoroughbred owned by the family, and the ponies are crossed with Shetlands to maintain their very small size. They are all under 7 hands in height, and are popular as children's pets. They are hardy and resourceful, friendly and intelligent. Some have been broken in for riding and driving.

Horses have been used for work on the land for centuries and, following the use of oxen, were the only form of work force available before the advent of the tractor and mechanized farming. All four of the heavy horses in Britain were used in this way — Suffolks, Shires, Clydesdales and Percherons. Suffolks were especially useful for working the heavy soil in East Anglia as they are clean-legged with no feather. Here, two Clydesdales are seen harrowing near Stirling in Scotland.

The Fell pony is a native of the Lake District, being found in Cumberland and Westmorland. Used in the eighteenth century as a pack pony for carting lead from the mines, he is now an all-round farm pony but has a good, sloping riding shoulder as well and can be successfully crossed with hunter or Thoroughbred blood. Compact and deep with plenty of bone, and very hardy, he is ideal for trekking and for long-distance rides. The height can vary between 13 and 14 hands and permitted colours are black, brown, dark bay and sometimes grey, preferably with no white markings.

The Derby, the most famous flat race, was first held in 1780. It is now run annually at Epsom on the first Wednesday in June over a distance of one and a half miles and is open to three-year-olds of either sex. The other two races which go to make up the 'Triple Crown' are the St Leger, run at Doncaster over one mile six furlongs, and the 2,000 Guineas, run at Newmarket over a mile. The other two classic races in England are the 1,000 Guineas and the Oaks, both open to fillies only. The racing Calendar goes back to 1727 and gives the pedigrees of the runners, all of which were of course Thoroughbreds; races for native ponies have no doubt been in existence for many centuries. Racing is now popular in many countries, particularly in France and the United States.

French Anglo-Arab

A breed based on very old Oriental blood, the French Anglo-Arab had a fresh infusion of Arab blood introduced in the early 1800s to replace the great losses incurred during the Revolution and the Napoleonic wars. Some forty years later the idea was developed of introducing English Thoroughbreds to the National Stud at Pompadour, and the mares there are now mated with Arab and Thoroughbred stallions alternately. Anglo-Arabs are bred at the Studs at Pau and Tarbes as well as at Pompadour and others in south-west France. They are usually 15.3 to 16 hands and may be any colour. Combining the best qualities of both breeds, they are used with considerable success in racing, eventing and show-jumping and make ideal all-round riding horses.

See also: Anglo-Arab.

French Arab

Arabs were introduced into France in the 1800s and are now principally bred at the National Stud of Tarber. They are very similar to the English Arab, having a short head, wide-set eyes, neck well set on sloping shoulders, tail set high and hard flat bone. They are usually chestnut, bay or grey in colour, averaging 15.2 to 16 hands. They are used with the Thoroughbred to produce the French Anglo-Arab.

See also: Arab, Desert Arab, Polish Arab, Shagya Arab.

The French Thoroughbred is a descendant of the English Thoroughbred, which in turn goes back to the Arab. The first French Thoroughbreds were imported from England primarily for racing when such racecourses as Longchamps and Deauville were set up. They are now bred principally at the National Stud of Pompadour, and America is a frequent purchaser of some of the most successful French stock. Apart from racing, the French Thoroughbred — along with its English counterpart — is, of course, used extensively for upgrading almost all other breeds.

See also: Australian Thoroughbred, Thoroughbred.

Friesian

A native of Holland, the Friesian is probably the oldest of our heavy breeds, although it had infusions of Andalusian and Oriental blood during the time of the Crusades. Great weight-carriers and good trotters, their popularity soon waned when they started to be bred for short, fast trotting races, and they were in danger of extinction before the First World War. A new society, however, saved the breed and now the Friesian is popular as a work horse and in harness. They are always black, stand about 15 hands, and are strong, active and willing workers. They have an abundance of mane, tail and feather and are very good-natured.

Gelderland

The Gelderland is found in Holland and is noted as an excellent carriage horse. It is also used for agricultural work, and when broken to saddle some have proved successful show-jumpers. They are usually grey or chestnut in colour, frequently with white markings on the face and legs, and average 15 to 16 hands. With their good sloping shoulders, and powerful quarters with the tail carried high, they are attractive horses with a rather high action.

The Golden Horseshoe Ride is run annually in Britain in different parts of the country. It is run on two consecutive days, a total of seventy-five miles being covered altogether: fifty miles on the first day and twenty-five miles on the second. To qualify for this event riders and horses have to complete one of the qualifying rides, of forty miles at a speed of 8 m.p.h., which are held during the year in various parts of the country. To gain a Golden Horseshoe the whole distance has to be covered at a minimum average speed of 9 m.p.h., and top marks for the veterinary examinations have to be gained. These examinations take place before the ride starts, in order to ensure that the competitors are in a fit condition to start; at the compulsory half-way check on the first day after twenty-five miles have been covered; at the end of the first day's ride; before the start of the second day and at the end of the second day. If a horse fails to reach the required standard of fitness it can be withdrawn at any stage. Any horse over 14 hands and over five years of age, whose owner is a member of the British Horse Society, may compete in this ride. It is one in which Arabs usually excel.

63

Descended from the East Anglian Norfolk Trotters, the early hackneys contained a certain amount of Thoroughbred blood, as one of the great influences on the breed was a sire descended from the Thoroughbred Flying Childers, whose name will be found in the General Stud Book. Infusions of Thoroughbred blood continued to be used during the 1800s, and the stud book rules still allow Thoroughbred crosses. The height limit is 15.3 hands; the predominant colours are bay, black and brown. Their high, free action is, of course, their main characteristic, and today they are most frequently seen between the shafts of a somewhat flimsy show-wagon, though at one time they were ridden as well as driven. The hackney must have hard feet and good limbs, combined with a strong back, loins and quarters. The shoulder should be sloping and set on to a medium-length neck with a quality head.

The Haflinger pony comes from the South Tyrol district of Austria, where their registration and organized breeding has been carried on for many years. All stallions in the Haflinger Stud Book go back to an Arab stallion named El Bedavi. They are tough and sure-footed mountain ponies, very strong and powerful, and in their native land they are used as all-round farm workers as well as for riding. The height can vary from 12.3 to 14.2 hands and they are always chestnut in colour with flaxen or silver manes and tails. No white markings on the legs are permitted but a white star or blaze is quite acceptable. They are very useful all-round ponies both to ride and to drive, and their placid temperaments make them especially suitable for beginners.

65

Hanoverian

A German breed, the Hanoverian was developed from Oriental, Neapolitan and later Holstein and Thoroughbred blood. It is similar to the Trakehner but somewhat heavier, and is frequently used in harness. Standing at 16 to 17 hands, they can be any whole colour and are strong with good action, often making successful show-jumpers.

The Highland's natural home is in northern Scotland and the Western Isles, particularly the Isle of Rhum. A breed of great antiquity, the Highland has in the past had an infusion of Arab blood. Originally bred for working the crofts and for carting deer, the Highland has become increasingly popular as a riding and trekking pony and combines strength and hardiness with an attractive head, wide-set eyes and a docile disposition. They can also be crossed successfully with Thoroughbreds to produce very useful hunters. The height varies between 13.2 to 14 hands; colours can be grey, bay, brown, dun with a characteristic eel stripe and chestnut with silver mane and tail.

Holstein

Bred principally in the Elmshorn area of West Germany, the Holstein is based on Oriental and Spanish horses crossed with native breeds. Later, Thoroughbred blood and that of the old Coach Horse, now known as the Cleveland Bay, was introduced and later still they were upgraded by the use of both German and English Thoroughbreds. Colours are usually bay, brown and black and the height is about 16 to 16.2 hands. Holsteins are now used extensively as all-round riding horses, excelling in show-jumping and eventing, and are also used in harness.

A hunter is, strictly speaking, a horse which can follow hounds across country, galloping over grassland and plough, jumping anything that comes in its path, and being up with hounds at the end of the day. The show hunter has to convey to the judge that it is capable of this performance by his near-perfect conformation, equable temperament and free-striding action at all paces. No jumping is demanded in the show ring except in working hunter classes. There are five classes for hunters: lightweight, for horses capable of carrying up to 12 st. 7 lbs; middleweight, 12 st. 7 lbs to 14 st.; heavyweight, over 14 st.; the small hunter, standing at 14.2 to 15.2 hands; and the ladies' hunter, which is usually ridden side-saddle.

Hunting is a traditional sport of the countryside. Foxhounds as we know them appeared in the sixteenth century (until this time any kind of dog was used). Deer and hare were the most popular quarry until the eighteenth century, when the fox began to be most frequently chased. To keep ahead of the faster, quality horses beginning to be bred, faster hounds were also bred and foxes also developed more speed. The 'Shires' of the Midlands provided the best and fastest hunting country. Today there are more hunts than ever before and more people ride to hounds, in spite of the increasing difficulties of getting across country because of motorways, railways, urbanization and barbed wire.

Icelandic pony

The Icelandic pony was introduced to Iceland in the ninth century by Norse settlers from Norway. It has since had infusions of Scottish blood, but for many years no new blood has been introduced. He stands at between 12 and 13 hands, is exceedingly hardy, strong, sturdy and good-natured and is always grey or dun. Primarily used for riding, the breed has a very comfortable ambling trot which covers a surprising amount of ground.

71

It is thought that the Irish Draught horse probably originated in Connemara, but that upon moving to other parts of Ireland it grew larger on the better feeding and grazing to be found. They are used for all sorts of farm work, and when crossed with Thoroughbred stallions make splendid hunters and show-jumpers with natural jumping ability. They are usually chestnut, bay, brown or grey in colour and the height varies between 15.2 and 16.2 hands. They are short, compact horses with good shoulders and legs with very little feather on them.

Jousting tournaments have recently been revived and exhibitions of chivalrous skills have been organized throughout the country by the British Jousting Association. The horses travel towards each other on either side of the 'tilt', the barrier dividing the two knights, at speeds of 25 to 30 m.p.h., and the idea is to thrust your opponent out of his saddle by the force of impact of your lance on his shield. The horses used are about 15.3 to 16.3 hands and are frequently half-breds. They must be of a calm and equable temperament so as not to be upset by all the noise and spectacle, but they must not be slugs either. Both knights and horses are decked out in the costume of the twelfth and thirteenth centuries; while the knights may occasionally get injured, the horses are never touched.

The predecessor of today's Jutland horse of Denmark is known to have featured in the twelfth century as a warhorse, and all through the Middle Ages they were extensively bred as weight-carrying chargers. They have always been popular as sturdy, active horses particularly well suited to heavy agricultural and draught work, but recently demand has dwindled considerably with the advent of mechanization.

The Kabardin is found in the Northern
Caucasia region of the USSR, some of
the best being bred at the Kabardino-
Balkarian autonomous republic stud
farms. Usually bay or black in colour and
about 15.2 hands, they have remarkable
powers of endurance and are very sure-
footed, being used as a means of
transport over the steep, rough cliff
tracks in the Caucasus.

Karabair

The Karabair is bred at collective stud farms at Uzbekistan and also at the Dzhizah Stud at Samarkand in Central Asia. It is probably derived from the Arab, from which it gets its powers of endurance and its exceptional soundness and agility. They are excellent all-round horses, being useful for light farm work as well as to ride and drive. They are also raced with a certain amount of success and are used for the mounted games which are popular in this part of the world. They average about 15.2 hands and are grey, bay or chestnut in colour.

Kazakh

A very ancient breed, the Kazakh was originally bred by nomads in the Kazakhstan region of the Russian steppes. They are exceptionally hardy and tough little horses and can live in great extremes of climate, often having to forage for themselves in deep snow and freezing temperatures. They excel as mounts for long-distance riding and are also used by the herdsmen. All colours are seen, the most common being bay, chestnut, black and grey, and they average 14.2 to 15 hands. In addition they are used for meat and the mares are milked.

Kisber

The Kisber Stud in Hungary is the principal stud for the breeding of half-bred horses and takes its name from the racehorse Kisber who won the Derby in 1876, among other races. Based on English Thoroughbred stallions, the Kisber type of half-bred averages 15.2 to 16.2 hands and is usually bay, brown, black or chestnut.

Kladruber

This Czechoslovakian breed takes its name from the Czechoslovakian government stud farm of Kladrub, which is the oldest stud in Europe. Ancestors of the Kladruber were the Spanish horses imported in the sixteenth century, but recently outcrosses with the Shagya Arabian have proved successful. Only black and grey — almost white — Kladrubers are now bred, but at one time bays, browns and chestnuts were also seen. Originally the Kladruber stood at 17.2 to 18 hands, and in teams of six or eight was used to draw the state coaches, black stallions being used to draw the funeral carriage and white stallions for festive occasions. They are now considerably smaller, being between 16 and 17 hands and are used for agricultural work as well as in harness. They have also had a certain amount of success as dressage horses.

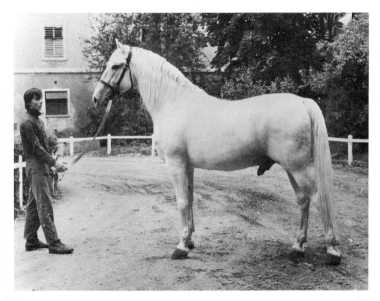

Based on the Spanish Andalusian, the Lippizaner is bred in many East European countries and in Austria. The Piber stud in Austria was started with six foundation stallions of different strains which persist today. The foals are born black and grow lighter with age; grey, brown, bay and chestnut Lippizaners are all seen. As well as their famed use in the Spanish Riding School at Vienna, Lippizaners are also driven and make excellent harness horses.

The Lippizaner is chiefly known for its connections with the Spanish Riding School in Vienna, where only the very best grey stallions can be used. They have large heads, thick, strong necks, loaded shoulders, powerful quarters and short legs; they vary in height between 14.3 and 16 hands. The stallion shown here is performing the *capriole*, perhaps the most difficult of all the 'airs above the ground'.

The Lusitanian is a native of Portugal and is almost exactly the same as the Andalusian of Spain. Usually grey in colour, they can also be chestnut, bay or black and stand between 15 and 16 hands. They have a small head set on to a rather thick neck, with good shoulders. They are strong and agile and have good, powerful quarters. Originally used in harness and for light farm work as well as for army remounts, they are now frequently trained for the Portuguese bull-ring. The *rejoneadore* must train his horse to an exceedingly high standard, as it is a disgrace for the horse ever to be touched by a bull, and imperfect training increases the dangers of the sport.

Mesohegyes

Like Kisber, Mesohegyes is one of the principal studs in Hungary, founded in 1784. These two studs, together with those at Babolna and Hortobagy, are the basis of breeding in Hungary. Hunter-type half-breds are produced at this stud, and all go back to the Thoroughbred stallions Furioso and North Star. They are used for all riding activities as well as in harness and can be bay, brown, black or grey in colour.

Mongolian Pony

The Mongolian pony is a direct descendant of the Przewalski horse which still exists in small numbers in the Gobi Desert. It is found all over Mongolia, Tibet and China and is raced in China, being exceedingly fast over short distances. These ponies have enormous powers of endurance and stamina and are usually about 13 to 14 hands in height. The most common colours are black, brown, bay or various shades of dun.

Morgan

The breed stems from one horse owned by Justin Morgan in Vermont at the end of the eighteenth century. He stood only about 14 hands high, but possessed a remarkable turn of speed as well as phenomenal strength and endurance. These qualities are maintained in the breed today, which is popular throughout the United States as a handsome and reliable all-purpose horse. Examples of the breed can frequently be seen in the show ring both under saddle and in harness.

Mounted Games

Gymkhana events are organized at a number of small shows throughout Britain, and some consist of nothing else. Events are normally divided by age limits, and are run in heats of four to six competitors. Musical sacks and sack races, flag races, bending, potato and obstacle races are all popular. A well-schooled pony is required; the best ones are small, fast and nippy. The Pony Club organizes an annual competition, known as the Prince Philip Cup, which culminates in a final held at the Horse of the Year Show at Wembley.

A mule is the offspring of a stallion donkey and a pony mare. They were used extensively abroad during the Second World War as a pack animal and as a way of transporting stores and equipment. They are capable of great endurance and can tolerate excessive changes in climate. There is a great variation in height – 12 to 17 hands but 14.2 hands is considered the maximum practical height for pack work. The back should be straight, the quarters muscular and the shoulder upright. The legs should be short and clean and the feet rather narrow and boxy. Two types of mule were recognized by the Army, the light draught type of 15 to 15.2 hands and the 'artillery pack' of 13.3 to 14.2 hands. The pace of mule transport was about 4 m.p.h. and 20 to 25 miles per day was the usual amount of ground covered. They are very sound and sure-footed and ideal for use on rough mountain tracks.

New Forest

Found in Hampshire in the south of England, this pony has inhabited the 60,000 acres of the New Forest for many hundreds of years, mention having been made of ponies in the Forest in Domesday Book in 1085. Over the centuries, however, a number of breeds have been introduced into the Forest including Arab, Thoroughbred, Fell and Welsh. The origins of this pony are therefore somewhat obscure, and there is no very definite and recognizable type. The size varies between 12 and 14.2 hands and they make ideal family ponies, being sound, tough and sure-footed as well as having a good riding shoulder. Any colour is acceptable except piebald and skewbald.

Normandy Half-bred

The Normandy half-bred, also known as the Anglo-Norman, is a descendant of the rather heavy Norman horse with many infusions of Thoroughbred blood. He is now an ideal riding horse, being especially suitable for show-jumping and cross-country work. The principal breeding area is the National Stud at Haras du Pin, but a heavier draught type, which has had infusions of Percheron blood, is bred in the de Mortagne region of France.

Norwegian

The Norwegian Fjord pony is very widely spread over the whole of Scandinavia and has inhabited Norway for many centuries — the Vikings bred ponies of this type. They are varying shades of dun with the black eel stripe down the back and black and silver mane, tail and legs. A small, compact pony of 13 to 14 hands, he is very strong and muscular, with a small head, powerful neck and short legs. He will do any work required of him and is especially useful for farm work and for work on mountain tracks.

A native of West Germany, the Oldenburg is based on the Friesian horse, but has had various importations of Spanish, Hanoverian, Cleveland Bay, Thorough-bred and Norman blood introduced over the centuries. The usual colours are bay, black, brown and grey and the height varies from 16.2 to 17.2 hands. They are strong, compact horses with good shoulders and plenty of bone, and are frequently used as carriage horses.

Orlov Trotter

The Orlov Trotter is one of the most popular of Russian breeds, being bred at a number of studs including the Moscow stud farm. He is the descendant of an Arab stallion and a Dutch mare and dates back to the end of the eighteenth century, but more recently the breed has had infusions of Thoroughbred, Arab and Danish blood. As well as being used for racing they are used in the upgrading of agricultural horses and also in harness. They are unusually sound and adaptable, and can be grey, black, chestnut or brown in colour. Their usual height is about 15.3 hands.

A pacer moves his legs laterally, the near fore and near hind moving alternately with the off fore and off hind. It is a very comfortable pace to ride at and one that covers maximum ground in the minimum time. Pacing and trotting races are very popular in the United States, New Zealand and Australia, more prize money being given for pacing races than trotting ones. It is also gaining popularity in Britain, with the Chacewater raceway near Walsall in Staffordshire as the spor''s headquarters. Following the American pattern, most of the races are for pacers. This three-year-old pacer is being exercised 'free-legged', that is, without the hobbles that are usually worn by pacers to accentuate their natural action. The world record for pacing over a mile, set up by Steady Star in 1971, is 1 min. 52 sec., about 33.06 m.p.h. This is only 2 m.p.h. slower than the Derby record set up by Mahmoud.

Palomino

The palomino in Britain is not a breed, but a type of horse or pony noted for the particular colour of its coat, the colour being that of 'a newly-minted gold coin'. The mane and tail should be pure white, not flaxen or silver, and white markings on the face and legs are permissible. Animals of this colouring may be of any size or shape; because of this lack of uniformity the palomino is unlikely to become an established breed in this country. The crosses most likely to produce this colouring are palomino × palomino, palomino × albino, chestnut × palomino and chestnut × albino, though these are not the only colours to get palomino. Foals tend to darken with age and it is by no means certain that a golden-coloured youngster will keep its colouring. Palominos are becoming increasingly popular, presumably because of their distinctive colouring, as Western pleasure horses.

Part-bred Arab

The part-bred Arab can cover a multitude of crosses, the part-bred register of the Arab Horse Society merely stipulating that there must be a minimum of $12\frac{1}{2}$ per cent Arab blood. Most part-breds are crossed with one or other of the native breeds, the most usually chosen probably being Welsh, New Forest, Connemara and Exmoor. A number of quality animals result from these crossings, the smaller ones probably appearing in the show ring as children's ponies while the larger ones, possibly crossed again with Thoroughbred, are seen in the ring as hacks. They do also, of course, frequently make very useful riding horses.

See also: Arab, Desert Arab, French Arab, Polish Arab.

Paso Fino

The Paso Fino is one of the oldest breeds and is bred principally in the region of Puerto Rico in South America. There are, however, about 500 of them in the United States, mostly in the eastern states. It is a natural pacer, having a four-beat gait [for which it is believed the Spanish jennet is responsible] and it moves in this manner right from birth, never having to be taught. There are several four-beat gaits: the *paso fino*, which is slow and collected, the *paso corto*, faster and used for trail riding, and the *paso largo*, the fastest gait. They are small, strong horses of about 14.3 hands, but they can travel quite easily at 12 to 15 m.p.h. and speeds of 20 m.p.h. are not unknown.

Percheron (1)

The original home of the Percheron is the La Perche region of northern France, from where it takes its name. It was bred to pull heavy coaches and artillery. It was introduced into Britain in 1916. The stallions must be at least 16.3 hands, and mares not less than 16.1 hands. Like the Suffolk Punch, they are clean-legged horses with no, or very little, feather on the heels of their rather short legs. The back should be short, shoulders well laid back, the neck thick and strong and with a wide, deep chest. The only permissible colours are grey or black, with a minimum of white markings. For its size and strength the Percheron is surprisingly active and agile.

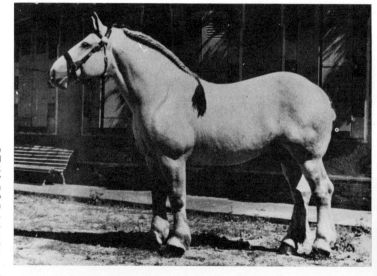

The Percheron is bred today in France on the borders of Normandy, Maine and Touraine, the mares being used to work the farms while the stallions are kept by a select few who control the breeding in the area. The best foals are sold only to the principal breeders. The Percheron still retains traces of its Arab ancestry, which can be seen in its good free action, suppleness and soundness. It is interesting to note the variations in type between the French and English Percheron, particularly with regard to the head.

Although the Pinto has its own breed society, the Pinto Horse Society of America, it is not a breed but a colour type similar to skewbald colouring. There are two types of coat pattern: the 'ovaro', a brown background coat colour with large white splashes, and the 'tobiano', predominantly white with splashes of brown. The Pinto has a reputation for toughness and endurance, and because of its ability to camouflage itself was much favoured by the American Indians. They are now used extensively in the United States as all-round riding horses and have proved their ability over fences.

There are now very few pit ponies left working in the mines, but Dartmoors, Shetlands, Welsh Mountain and Icelandic ponies were used extensively at one time for pulling coal trucks. In the mines with higher workings Exmoors and Fells were also used. The Pit Ponies Protection Society was founded in 1927 with the object of improving conditions underground for ponies and with the eventual aim of abolishing their use.

Police Horse

The training establishment at the Metropolitan Branch of the Mounted Police is at Imber Court, Surrey and has been in operation since 1920. A form of mounted police goes back to 1758, when two horses were attached to Bow Street, and forty-seven years later a Bow Street Horse Patrol was formed. Most of the horses are bought in Yorkshire, usually unbroken. They are generally of hunter type, probably three-quarter-breds with good, hard bone and excellent feet. They must have a calm temperament and not be lacking in courage. The special police training lasts about six months and includes nuisance training as well as the acceptance of heavy traffic. A new recruit is here seen negotiating steep steps during his Imber Court training.

Polish Arab

The most famous Polish Arab sire of all time must surely be the pure white stallion Showroneck, who was bred at Poland's Janow stud and was imported to Britain in 1913 where he eventually stood at the famous Crabbet Park stud. The first Arab studs were started in the early sixteenth century, but war seems to have ravaged Poland's studs and decimated the horse world and it is only during the past twenty years that the studs have built up their population and restarted selective breeding. More recently Grojec [shown here], Gerwazy and Karramba are the sires who have had the most influence on the breed. The height ranges from 14.2 to 15.2 hands, and permitted colours are grey, chestnut and bay.

See also: Desert Arab, French Arab, Shagya Arab.

Polo Pony

Polo was introduced into Britain from India in the nineteenth century by British officers serving in India, and its popularity soon spread all over the world. Small hunter-type ponies of about 14.2 hands were the favourite mounts for polo, but in 1918 the height limit was abolished and a bigger pony of about 15.1 hands was the favoured height. The prime requisites for polo ponies are a good turn of speed, stamina, courage, balance, the ability to 'turn on a sixpence' and an equable temperament. It is easier to hit the ball from a short-striding pony than from a pony with a longer stride, and the former are therefore preferred.

Przewalski Horse

The Przewalski horse is one of the ancestors of our present-day breeds, and it is still found in very small numbers in the west of the Gobi Desert in Mongolia. The horses have changed very little since the Ice Ages. They are 12 to 14 hands high, are various shades of dun in colour with a mealy muzzle and a black dorsal stripe, black mane and tail and frequently zebra markings on the legs. An explorer by the name of Colonel N. M. Przewalski first discovered a few of these horses in 1881, on the edge of the Gobi Desert. There are thought to be only about forty animals living in a wild state, though about a hundred are kept in captivity in various zoos in Europe and the United States.

About seventy years ago Exmoor stock was introduced to the Quantock range of hills in the West Country. Some years later three registered stallions – a New Forest-cross-Arab and two Welsh-cross-Arabs – were run on the Quantocks and the resultant stock on the hills are now known as Quantock ponies. They are usually bay and brown in colour, but greys and chestnuts are also found. They combine the hardiness of the Exmoor with the good looks of the Arab, from whom they tend to inherit a slightly dished face. Averaging 14.2 hands in height, they are very versatile, and have proved useful ponies for children to compete in hunter trials and for jumping.

Quarter Horse

The Quarter Horse gets its name from the match races that were once run in the United States. They took place over a distance of about a quarter of a mile, usually through the main street of the town. More recently the Quarter Horse has become popular as a rodeo horse. They have extraordinary 'cow-sense' and are thus valuable mounts for the cattlemen. The height varies between 15.2 and 16 hands, and any colour is recognized. They are noted for their powerful quarters, strong back, sloping shoulders, short, wide head and strong legs with plenty of bone.

106

Riding Pony

Descended from small Thoroughbred polo pony stallions crossed with native pony mares, principally of Welsh and Dartmoor breeding, the riding pony is a fairly recent development. The show pony should have superb conformation, with very good riding shoulders, well set on to a medium-length neck and a quality head, fairly wide between the eyes. The legs should be clean and hard with short cannon bones, the action free — straight from the shoulder in front and well engaged behind. Like the hack, the show pony must have the essential 'presence'. Arabs have recently been siring native pony mares for the show ring, but in general this has not been as successful as the Thoroughbred matings. The show ring caters for three heights of classes for ponies: under 12.2 hands, 12.2 to 13.2 hands and 13.2 to 14.2 hands.

107

Rodeo

Rodeos were originally a rounding-up of cattle on the prairies in the United States. Now, however, the word has come to mean a show at which cowboys give displays of calf-roping, and compete with each other in riding bucking broncos or buckjumpers. True buckjumpers are only found among the ranch horses of the USA and Australia, but bucking straps, fixed to the 'dee' rings at the back of the saddle, are passed under the horse's belly and are fastened tightly to induce him to arch his back and jump into the air, taking all four feet off the ground at once and thus getting rid of his rider.

Originally known as the North-West Mounted Police, the Mounties were formed to keep the peace on the north-west frontier of Canada. The horses are now bred at the Fort Walsh stud, which was founded in 1940, and are between 15.3 and 16.3 hands in height. Only black or brown horses are used and they must have good quarters and short backs. They are usually foaled out of a half-bred mare by a Thoroughbred stallion.

Shagya Arab

The Shagya Arab is bred principally at the Babolna stud in Hungary, but they are also bred in Czechoslovakia. They have been successfully crossed with the Kladruber to improve the quality of the latter. They stand at about 15 hands and are nearly always grey in colour with a silky coat. The head is small, with a slightly dished profile and wide-set eyes and is well set on to an arched neck and sloping shoulder.

See also: Arab, Desert Arab, French Arab, Polish Arab.

Shetland

The Shetland is the smallest of our native mountain and moorland breeds, varying from 32 to 42 inches at the wither. His original habitat is the Shetland and Orkney Islands. A utility pony, suitable for working the crofts as well as for riding and driving, the breed is very hardy and strong for its size and at one time was used for work in the pits. If properly trained, and not allowed to become too fat, they make good riding ponies for children. With a short, strong back, deep through the girth, with short hard legs and a mass of mane and tail, the Shetland can be any colour.

Descended from the English Great Horse of the Middle Ages, the Shire is principally found in Lincolnshire, Cambridgeshire, Huntingdonshire and the northern counties of England. Standing anything up to 18 hands, the Shire is usually black, brown, bay or grey in colour, usually with white markings on the face and white socks with an abundance of silky feather. He is exceptionally docile, powerful and possessed of great stamina, with a short, muscular back and loins, deep body and clean-cut, hard legs. His original job, in Elizabethan days, was to carry the knights in armour and later to work on the land. He is perhaps the best example of equine magnificence.

Show Hack

The show hack is the supreme quality riding horse, combining impeccable manners with outstanding action and indefinable 'presence'. He must give an appearance of tremendous elegance and be balanced, level and controlled while moving freely at all paces. Although this paragon is a type and not a breed, he is almost always of Thoroughbred, Arab or Anglo-Arab breeding. The shoulder should be well laid back, the head fine and neat, and he should have a good length of rein. There are three classes for hacks: small hacks of 14.2 to 15 hands; large hacks, 15 to 15.3 hands; and ladies' hacks, from 14.2 to 15.3 hands, which are usually shown side-saddle.

Show-jumper

Show-jumping is undoubtedly the most popular of our equine pastimes in terms of both competitor and spectator appeal. There is no fixed type or breed of show-jumper and it is not always the better bred Arabs and Thoroughbreds who win top honours. Attempts have been made to breed in jumping blood but so far not with any success. As with eventing, the horse must have plenty of courage to tackle big fences and a will to win and this is far more important than his make and shape, though obviously a horse with good conformation is less likely to suffer from strains, etc.

Spotted Horses

Although the same markings can occur in both spotted and Appaloosa horses, the two should not be confused. Spotted markings can occur on any breed — the name only means a colour type. Three different types of markings are recognized: 'blanket' is the term applied to spots of any colour on a white back or quarters; 'leopard' denotes spots appearing on a white or light-coloured coat; and 'snow-flake' describes white spots on a darker-coloured coat.

Raised extensively in Kentucky, the Standardbred is popular all over the United States and Canada and is the official name for both trotters and pacers. The breed goes back to Hambletonian 10, who was foaled in 1849, and through him to Messenger, a Thoroughbred imported to America in 1788, and a Norfolk Trotter mare, Bellfounder. Ninety per cent of all Standardbreds go back to Hambletonian 10. The name Standardbred is derived from the custom of testing harness racers to see whether they could complete a mile within the standard time. They are slightly smaller than the pacers and trotters being bred in England, averaging 15.2 hands, and they can be any colour. They must have strength, stamina and exceptionally good legs and feet.

Steeplechasing

The first recorded steeplechase was run over three miles at Bedford in 1810. There were eight fences and the race was run in heats, the winner being Fugitive. The first organized meeting was run at St Albans, Hertfordshire in 1830. Seven years later the Grand National was founded at Aintree over four miles 856 yards but it was not known by that name until 1847. The National has thirty fixed fences, of which the best known is Becher's Brook, shown here.

Suffolk Punch

The Suffolk Punch, a native of East Anglia since the early 1500s, is the smallest of our heavy horse breeds, standing only about 16 hands. He is always chestnut in colour, varying in shade from a bright reddish chestnut to a very dark brownish colour. A small amount of white marking is permissible on the face but no socks or stockings are allowed. He has a rather large, thick head, short legs with very little feather and large feet. The quarters should be strong and powerful and the body compact and deep. Essentially a farm horse, he is reported to be one of the fastest workers, and especially suited to working the heavy East Anglian soil. He is also used by certain breweries for pulling drays.

Like polo, tent pegging originated in India, being practised by the army. A peg, usually painted white, is pushed into the ground at an angle with about eight inches sticking up, and has to be stabbed and carried at the gallop on the end of a lance. This exercise is now carried out at displays given by the army and the police.

Thoroughbred

The Thoroughbred, the fastest horse in the world, is descended from the three Arabian sires imported into England in the late seventeenth and early eighteenth centuries, and all Thoroughbreds entered in the General Stud Book go back to one of them. They are the Byerley Turk, the Darley Arabian and the Godolphin Arabian. Essentially, the Thoroughbred is a racehorse but he may also be seen as a hunter, eventer, show-jumper, dressage horse and so on and is frequently crossed with native breeds to add quality. The head should be fine, the eye intelligent and the neck of a good length. The shoulder should be sloping, the cannon bones short, and the quarters well-rounded. Action should be free and straight and he should move with long, low strides. Usual colours are bay, brown, black, grey and chestnut.

See also: Australian Thoroughbred, French Thoroughbred.

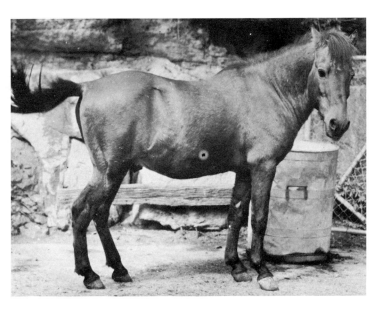

The Timor pony is a native of the Island of Timor off the north-west coast of Australia. Because of their remarkable hardiness and stamina they were imported into Western Australia in the nineteenth century, and their influence later spread throughout the Australian mainland. They are usually dark in colour, and remarkably agile for their small size of about 12 hands.

The best Toric horses are bred at the Toric state farm in the Estonian area of the USSR. They developed from an imported Norfolk Roadster stallion put to native mares, and later more Roadsters and Orlov Trotters were introduced. They are exceedingly strong and powerful and capable of carrying and pulling great weights. They average 15.2 to 16 hands, and have good action, short legs and equable temperaments.

Trakehner

The Trakehner or East Prussian horse was first bred at the stud of Trakehnen, which was founded in 1732 in East Prussia. Based on Oriental blood, English Thoroughbreds were introduced at the beginning of the nineteenth century, the aim being to breed quality horses suitable for agricultural purposes as well as for cavalry remounts. They are now used extensively as all-round riding horses and also in harness. Their average height is 16 to 16.2 hands and they can be any whole colour. Quality horses with good action, sloping shoulders and strong quarters, they frequently make good jumpers.

Trekking has become increasingly popular as a holiday pastime in recent years, and a number of centres have been set up all over Britain and also abroad. It is an ideal way of seeing the countryside, some of the best parts of which are inaccessible by any other means. As the majority of trekking parties go about 12 to 15 miles a day and do not go out of a walk, trekking can be a holiday for complete beginners, but some centres organize post trekking as well for riders with a little more experience. This means that the party does not return to base each night, but stays overnight at a prearranged spot and continues from there the following day. The distances covered on these trips, about 20 to 25 miles a day often with trotting and cantering included, are considered to be too much for complete beginners. The ponies being used in this photograph are all Highlands, but New Forest ponies, Connemaras, Welsh ponies, cobs and Dartmoors are all used, together with cross-breds, depending on the part of the country visited.

Trotter

The National Harness Racing Club, chaired by Lord Langford who breeds both trotters and pacers at his North Wales stud, controls harness racing in Britain. There are between 400 and 500 horses currently in training and both trainers and drivers must all be licensed. Trotting horses tend to mature later than pacers and they are not so fast. Neither do they wear hobbles for racing, although they do frequently break the trot. When this happens in a race the driver must pull back, and consequently loses ground.

Tskhenburti

Riding for pleasure in the USSR is a fairly recent development, but at the Hippodrome in the Ukrainian capital of Kiev traditional national games are staged regularly. One of the oldest ones, which has been played in Russia for over 1,000 years, is *Tskhenburti*, a sort of tennis on horseback.

The Tushin is bred in the upland, mountainous regions of the USSR and is ideal for use on the narrow tracks and passes over the mountains, being extremely sure-footed, sound and hardy. He is usually black, brown or bay in colour and averages 14.2 to 15 hands.

127

Waler

The Australian Waler, named after the first colony of New South Wales, has a reputation for soundness and endurance and was much in demand for cavalry remounts. During the First World War more than 120,000 horses were exported for the Allied armies in India, Africa, Palestine and Europe, but with a diminishing demand the breeders of Walers are now concentrating upon the lighter bloodstock types. Walers can be any colour; the height is usually about 16 hands. Their principal use today is as police horses.

Welsh Mountain

The Welsh Mountain pony, Section A in the Welsh Pony and Cob Society Stud Book, has been bred on the mountains of Wales since Roman days, although there have since been infusions of Arab, Thoroughbred and hackney blood. Intelligent, with a fine head, dished profile, large eye and prick ears, these ponies are probably the most beautiful of the British native breeds. They are sound and hardy, with true pony character and good action. They provide very good children's ponies, having a good sloping riding shoulder, and are the ideal foundation stock for breeding quality show ponies. They are strong and versatile, being as suitable to drive as to ride. The height limit is 12 hands; permissible colours are chestnut, grey, brown, bay, black, cream or dun.

The Welsh Section B is the riding pony of the Welsh breeds, the supreme pony of the show ring. Not exceeding 13.2 hands, his attributes are very similar to those of the Welsh Mountain pony, but he must have quality riding pony character and action. However, substance and hardiness must not be forsaken in an effort to breed in 'quality' and exclusive Thoroughbred needs are to be discouraged at all costs. They are, however, very successfully crossed with small Arabs or Thoroughbreds to produce the larger 14.2 hands show ponies, and the best ones can command very high prices. A strong sloping shoulder is a necessity, as is a neat head set on to a neck of suitable length. Strong limbs are essential, as are good quarters, and the tail should be set high and carried gaily. Any colour is permissible except piebald and skewbald.

Welsh Pony of Cob Type

The Welsh Pony of cob type, Section C, is the smaller edition of the Welsh Cob, and has a height limit of 13.2 hands. Excellent to ride and to drive, he is very versatile, combining strength with quality and common sense. He makes a very good small hunter, having all the qualities of the larger Cob. He is strong, sturdy and 'stuffy', and should have an abundance of pony character. His well laid back shoulder and good length of rein make him a comfortable ride; his powerful quarters and muscular thigh, allied to good bone, ensure that he can carry a fair amount of weight for a day's hunting without due strain in any but fast grassland country. The mane and tail should be silky, not coarse or wiry, as should the small amount of feather on the heels. Any colour is permitted except piebald and skewbald.

131

The Welsh Cob, Section D, is probably based on 'the old Welsh carthorse', but it is not clear exactly what that was. However, mention of something sounding very similar to the present-day Cob was made as long ago as the fourteenth century. The largest and strongest of the Welsh breeds, the Cob is as good under the saddle as in harness, and has all the natural fire, courage and action of the Welsh breeds. Standing from 14.2 to 15.2 hands, they can gallop and jump and are the ideal riding horse, combining active strength with quality and an equable temperament. When crossed with Thoroughbred blood, they produce very useful hunters up to a considerable weight. Any colour except piebald and skewbald is permitted.

Wielkopolski

The Wielkopolski is bred in the region known as Greater Poland, principally at the Polish government stud farm at Racot. It has been developed from Oriental, Hanoverian and Thoroughbred blood, and later Trakehner stallions were introduced as well. The heavier specimens are used for agricultural work while the lighter ones are ideal both to ride and to drive. Any whole colour is recognized, and the height is usually about 16 hands.

The Olympic Games

Horses first appeared in chariot races in the 25th Olympiad, held in 680 BC. The Games were abolished in AD 393, and it was not until some years after their revival at the end of the nineteenth century that equestrian events were again included. It is largely thanks to Count Clarence von Rosen and his Swedish compatriots that they formed part of the 1908 Games, which took place in London.

The first Olympic competitions for horses varied from one competition to the next. Three separate equestrian activities are now included: dressage, show-jumping and combined training (the three-day event). Until after the Second World War the scene was dominated by the cavalry. The upsurge of civilian riding immediately after the war occurred all over the world, and competitors in military uniform are now in a minority.

The dressage competition is still a specialist activity, but the show-jumping and combined training events are immensely popular 'spectator sports'.

Olympic Games results

1948 London
Dressage: 1 France 2 USA 3 Portugal
Three-day event: 1 USA 2 Sweden 3 Mexico
Show jumping: 1 Mexico 2 Spain 3 Great Britain

1952 Helsinki
Dressage: 1 Sweden 2 Switzerland 3 Germany
Three-day event: 1 Sweden 2 Germany 3 USA
Show jumping: 1 Great Britain 2 Chile 3 USA

1956 Stockholm
Dressage: 1 Sweden 2 Germany 3 Switzerland
Three-day event: 1 Great Britain 2 Germany
  3 Canada
Show jumping: 1 Germany 2 Italy 3 Great Britain

1960 Rome
Dressage: No team awards
Three-day event: 1 Australia 2 Switzerland 3 France
Show jumping: 1 Germany 2 USA 3 Italy

1964 Tokyo
Dressage: 1 Germany 2 Switzerland 3 USSR
Three-day event: 1 Italy 2 USA 3 Germany
Show jumping: 1 Germany 2 France 3 Italy

1968 Mexico
Dressage: 1 Germany 2 USSR 3 Switzerland
Three-day event: 1 Great Britain 2 USA 3 Australia
Show jumping: 1 Canada 2 France 3 Germany

1972 Munich
Dressage: 1 USSR 2 Germany 3 Sweden
Three-day event: 1 Great Britain 2 USA 3 Germany
Show jumping: 1 Germany 2 USA 3 Italy

Index

Australia

Australian Thoroughbred
Brumby
Timor pony
Waler

China

Mongolian pony
Przewalski

Eastern Europe

Kisber
Kladruber
Lippizaner
Mesohegyes
Polish Arab
Shagya Arabian
Wielkopolski

France

Breton
Camarguais
French Anglo-Arab
French Arab

French Thoroughbred
Normandy half-bred
Percheron

Germany and Austria

Haflinger
Hanoverian
Holstein
Lippizaner
Oldenburg
Trakehner

Great Britain

Anglo-Arab
Arab
Cleveland Bay
Clydesdale
Cob
Connemara
Dales
Dartmoor
Exmoor
Fell
Hackney
Highland

Hunter
Irish Draught
New Forest
Part-bred Arab
Quantock pony
Riding pony
Shetland
Shire
Show hack
Suffolk punch
Thoroughbred
Trotter
Welsh Mountain (Section A)
Welsh Section B
Welsh Section C
Welsh Cob (Section D)

Holland and Belgium

Ardennes
Friesian
Gelderland

Middle East

Caspian pony
Desert Arab

Scandinavia

Icelandic pony
Jutland
Norwegian pony

South America

Falabella
Paso Fino

Spain and Portugal

Alter-Real
Andalusian
Lusitanian

United States

American Saddlebred
Appaloosa
Cutting horse
Morgan
Pinto
Quarter Horse
Standardbred

USSR

Akhal-teke
Bashkir
Budjonny
Don
Kabardin
Karabair
Kazakh
Orlov Trotter
Toric
Tushin

International types

Donkey
Mule
Palomino
Spotted horses

Activities and sports

Cavalry
Circus horse
Dressage
Driving
Eventing
Farm horse

Flat racing
Golden Horseshoe ride
Hunting
Jousting
Mounted Games
Pacing
Pit ponies
Police horse
Polo pony
Rodeo
Royal Canadian Mounted Police
Show-jumping
Steeplechasing
Tent pegging
Trekking
Tskhenburti

Acknowledgements

The author and publishers would like to express their thanks to the owners of photographs reproduced in this book:

Australian News & Information Bureau, for pages 32, 121, 128; Authenticolor, 82; Findlay Davidson, 119; Deford Studio, 96; Fiona Forbes, 72, 120; Foto-Bureau 'Sport', 61; Fox Photos, 36, 57, 87, 117; French Tourist Office, London, 34; Freudy Photos, 23; Jean Froissard, 8, 31, 58, 59, 60, 89, 98; Kit Houghton, 105; Ann Hyland, 99, 116; Keystone, 54, 74, 104; Leslie Lane, frontispiece, 25, 27, 39, 40, 41, 42, 43, 45, 46, 49, 50, 51, 52, 53, 62, 63, 64, 65, 66, 67, 68, 69, 80, 81, 86, 88, 90, 91, 93, 94, 95, 101, 102, 103, 107, 111, 112, 113, 114, 115, 118, 124, 129, 130, 131, 132; Mrs Mackay-Smith, 78, 79, 83, 110, 123, 133; Elsa Mayo, 35; Ern McQuillan, 29; Frank H. Meads, 70; Novosti, 21, 30, 33, 48, 75, 76, 77, 84, 92, 126, 127; Peter Roberts, 26, 44, 106; Udo Schmidt, 50; The Scotsman, 100; Sport & General, 37, 38, 56, 97; Tunbridge Wells Advertiser, 125; Marylian Watney, 85.